To Pippa + Stewart,

For both of you in ___ months of being in your ___ to!

As life moves forward - so does this book - it was given to me but I sense it will have a place on your bookshelf as a fond memory of time passing in Canberra

xx your neighbours

Marg, Alan + Chamois (Chammie 🐾)

7/2/13

the CAPITAL COOKBOOK

zorana grbic

photography jeremy rozdarz

acknowledgments

I have been extraordinarily lucky in achieving my dream of publishing this book.
Most of all in working with people who shared my dream.

Jeremy, a photographer whose talent and complete dedication have brought us images that this city and its people deserve.

Anne, who has shared my vision with equal commitment and passion and whose skills in production have turned a dream into a book.

Linda and Todd whose tireless effort and professionalism have brought vision to print.

A special thankyou to all the Chefs for sharing their secrets with us.

Thank you for the laughs and memories.
Most of all I have been lucky in being able to call this city my home.

Publisher: Abalholt Pty Limited
Photographer/Design: Jeremy Rozdarz
Editorial Director: Anne Macafee
Production: Todd Hayward

Published by: Abalholt Pty Limited
Printed by: National Capital Printing, Canberra, ACT

Text ©Zorana Grbic
Photographs ©Jeremy Rozdarz

Tulips photos page 32, Captain Cook fountain photo page 69, ©Kate Patrick
Photograph of Jeremy ©Nathan Higgins

National Library of Australia Cataloguing-in-Publication
ISBN: 0-646-43799-2

1. Cookery - Australian Capital Territory - Canberra
2. Restaurants - Australian Capital Territory - Canberra
3. Canberra (A.C.T)
641.599471

All rights reserved. No part of this publication may be reproduced, stored in a retrieval system or transmitted in any form by any means without the prior permission in writing of the publishers.

Available through: thecapitalcookbook@hotmail.com

contents

5 introduction

12 spring

46 summer

78 autumn

112 winter

144 notes

145 restaurant index

145 photo index

146 recipe index

Canberra, an aboriginal word for Meeting Place, has certainly lived up to its name for me. Canberra has been my home for the past 24 years.

With this book I have been indulged and certainly privileged in being able to combine two of my favourite pleasures, continually discovering the beauty of this city and its cuisine.

I am forever amazed at the extraordinary vision of choosing an unforgiving land, and turning it into a stunning city resting around the lakeshores.

I have now rediscovered the enormous beauty of Canberra, this time through the lens of a talented photographer who as you will see has captured images of Canberra which show it as "city with soul", full of natural beauty, world standard culture and art and a sense of community that fulfils our essential need of belonging.

I have combined all of this with another pleasure that can warm up your soul—Good Food! Some of Canberra's celebrated chefs have opened their kitchen doors and shared their secrets with us. Real masters of their profession and larger than life characters they are the true hosts of Canberra.

By letting me into their world for such a brief moment I have witnessed the enormous complexity of their profession. They handle the pressure with such grace and ease that I now see that they are maestros of the kitchen.

Some of the memorable experiences were at Belluci's Woden where Frank defies gravity and I am yet to see his feet touch the floor. The Green Herring appears from the outside like a rambling cottage from yesteryear. But it is once you enter, taste Graham's food and listen to him "talk food" that you are transported into a truly seductive atmosphere. Milk & Honey's Miriana, is as smooth and sweet as the name suggests. She welcomes guests with a smile that can light up a city block. James in the lush surroundings of Aubergine and Courgette is serene and confident as the "King of Food" should be.

One last indulgence. I have shared with you a recipe my grandmother used to make. Simple, yet deliciously indulgent in an old fashioned way. In a family of girls I was lucky to inherit her cookbook. As in her cookbook, I have left a few pages at the back for notes so that you can jot down places you might like to visit, food to cook and friends to invite!

Enjoy!

The Bush Capital

The Capital

we have opened the doors to the kitchens

of canberra's finest restaurants…

spring

oven roasted fillet of barramundi on a fennel and orange salad

1 kg large barramudi fillet (skin on)
1 tablespoon olive oil
sea salt
freshly ground black pepper
½ large fennel bulb
1 orange cut into segments
2 cups fine grade mesclun

dressing
1 cup extra virgin olive oil
1 teaspoon seeded Dijon mustard
1 teaspoon red wine vinegar
sea salt
freshly ground black pepper

Trim barramundi and cut into 4 even portions.

To make dressing, blend all ingredients together.

Remove the core from the fennel and slice thinly. Place in a bowl with the orange segments, seasoning and 2 tablespoons of the dressing.

Heat a heavy based oven proof pan over high heat and add a tablespoon of olive oil. Place the barramundi skin side down and cook until golden and crisp. Turn barramundi fillet over and place in oven at 220°c for approximately 8 minutes, until cooked.

While the barramundi is cooking add the mesclun to the orange and fennel in the bowl and coat all leaves with dressing.

Place the salad evenly over 4 plates then place the barramundi fillet on top. Dress the plate with more dressing and serve.
Serves 4

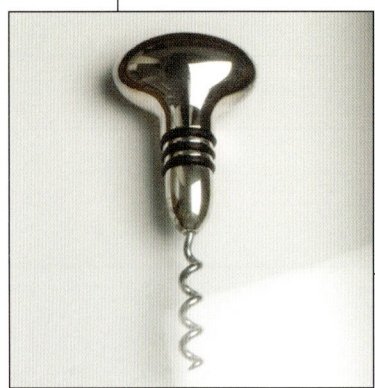

Anise

tuna tartare

base

1 firm black eggplant
2 truss tomatoes, peeled
30 ml red wine vine vinegar
1 teaspoon sugar
½ teaspoon salt
pinch ground black pepper
½ teaspoon chopped garlic
60 ml extra virgin olive oil
1 bunch roquette

sauce

30 ml quality japanese mirin
20 ml salt reduced soy sauce

tuna mix

320 g 'A' grade tuna
   (sliced with the grain
   into 2 x 1cm strips)
1 spanish onion finely diced
½ red birds eye chilli
1 teaspoon finely chopped ginger
10 fresh basil leaves finely sliced
pinch salt
pinch sugar
pinch fresh ground pepper
1 teaspoon small capers

base

Peel eggplant and cut into 1cm rounds (you need 8 slices), sprinkle with a little salt and place in a colander to extract bitterness. Wash and pat dry with a cloth, dust in flour and shallow fry in olive oil until golden. Place on a baking tray in stacks of two. Blend tomato, garlic, vinegar, season with sugar, salt and pepper. Pass mixture through a sieve and pour liberally on top of eggplant stacks. Drizzle with extra virgin olive oil and bake at 180°c until golden (approx 20 mins). Allow to cool at room temperature

sauce

Mix ingredients together

tuna mix

Mix all ingredients together carefully with a spoon. Add sauce. Check balance of flavours and adjust if required.

to serve

Toss roquette with a little extra virgin olive oil, salt and ground black pepper. Place a small amount in the centre of the plate. Place the eggplant stacks on top of the roquette. Carefully place the tuna on top of the eggplant trying to get as much height as you can. Drizzle a little extra virgin olive oil over the top and sprinkle a few capers and crack a little black pepper on and around the stacks. Serves 4

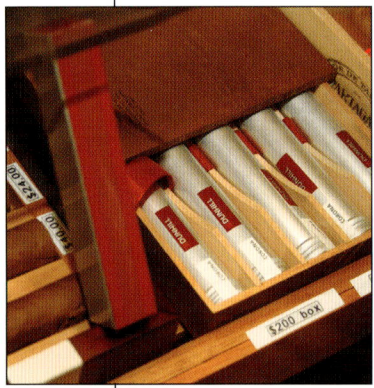

Ottoman

grilled chermoula marinated cod in vine leaves with cucumber and chilli dipping sauce

250 g blue eye cod fillet
5 vine leaves in brine (soaked in fresh water overnight)

chermoula
1 small spanish onion
1 bunch continental parsley
1 bunch coriander
3 cloves garlic
3 teaspoon ground cumin
3 teaspoon ground coriander
2 teaspoon paprika
pinch cayenne pepper
juice ½ lemon
½ cup olive oil
pinch saffron
½ teaspoon tumeric
2 teaspoon salt

dipping sauce
¼ cup white vinegar
2 teaspoon sugar
½ lebanese cucumber (seeded) finely diced
¼ teaspoon chopped red chilli

Cut fish into 4 cm x 2 cm pieces, marinate in chermoula overnight.

Pat dry the vine leaves and wrap the fish pieces. Char grill the fish in vine leaves, turning often. Allow to rest and cut in half. Serve cut side up with dipping sauce on the side.

chermoula
Puree all ingredients in a food processor.

dipping Sauce
Combine vinegar, sugar and chilli in a saucepan. Heat until sugar dissolves. Simmer for 2 minutes. Chill and stir in diced cucumber.

Bookplate

pistachio crumbed lamb rack served with sweet potato mash

lamb rack
4 x 4 lamb racks
1 cup breadcrumbs
1 cup pistachio
egg wash for crumbing
flour

sweet potato mash
large sweet potato
100 ml cream
50 g butter
sea salt
freshly ground black pepper

lamb rack
Crush pistachio in food processor, leaving fairly coarse. Toast in a moderate oven for 5–10 minutes. Combine pistachio and crumbs. Double crumb lamb racks in pistachio mix

Coat lamb lightly in oil and roast in hot (180°–200°c) oven for 10–15 minutes. Rest for 5 minutes, keeping warm. Slice and serve on sweet potato mash with steamed green vegetables.

sweet potato mash
Peel and dice sweet potato. Place in a large pot, cover with salted water and boil till tender. In a separate pot, boil cream and butter with salt and pepper, and reduce by half. Strain sweet potato, add cream and butter, blend in a food processor to a smooth paste.
Serves 4

Milk and Honey

roast vegetable stack with polenta on creamed leeks and cannelini beans

selection of seasonal vegetables

polenta
500 g polenta
1 litre water or milk
½ litre chicken stock
2 bay leaves
salt
pepper

creamed leeks & cannelini beans
1 tablespoon garlic
3 leeks cut into ½ moons
500 g cannelini beans
150 g butter
2 sticks celery
300 ml white wine
½ bunch parsley
¼ litre chicken stock

roquette pesto
2 huge handfuls roquette
100 g pine nuts
½ bunch parsley
150 g parmesan
sea salt
freshly ground black pepper
olive oil

garlic aioli
2 eggs
1 tablespoon roasted garlic
1 tablespoon dijon mustard
500 ml olive oil
sea salt
freshly ground black pepper

vegetables
Thinly slice vegetables, lightly coat in olive oil, season, place on a tray and roast in a 170°c oven until cooked

polenta
Bring liquids and bay leaves to the boil. Whisk in polenta until combined, lightly season. Simmer for 30–45 minutes, remove the bay leaves and check if further seasoning required. Place on a tray in a thin layer to cool. Once cooled cut into squares.

creamed leeks and cannelini beans
Sweat celery, leek and garlic in butter. Add the beans and wine reducing for 2 minutes. Add chicken stock and simmer slowly until the beans soften and the sauce thickens, remove from heat. Add parsley and season once cooled

roquette pesto
In a mortar and pestle blend roquette, pine nuts, parsley, parmesan, salt and pepper, once blended, slowly add enough olive oil to make a paste.

garlic aioli
Combine garlic, mustard and eggs in a food processor, add oil slowly to form a light mayonnaise, season and adjust consistency with water if necessary.

to serve
Pour a ladle full of creamed leeks and cannelini beans onto a plate. Place one layer of vegetables on the leeks and beans and then place a dollop of pesto and aioli on top, repeat vegetable layering to form a stack. Arrange a square of polenta on top of stack with a final dollop of aioli and pesto.

Verve

seared 'spring bay' scallops with jerusalem artichokes, crisp speck and sauternes butter sauce

10 scallops
10 slices jerusalem artichokes (1cm thick peeled)
100 g spinach
3 pieces speck, thinly sliced
1 punnet mache
1 small head frizzay
2 tablespoons aioli
60 ml sauternes
50 g butter
fine herbs
1 lemon
house dressing

Place speck on baking tray in oven at 120°c and leave for 25 minutes or until crisp. Pick and wash the salad. Pan fry artichokes in butter until golden and tender, remove from pan and drain.

Reduce sauternes by half and monter with butter until it reaches coating consistency. Add fine herbs and season to taste.
Season scallops. Heat pan until smoking, then add one tablespoon of oil. Place scallops in pan and cook until golden on one side. Turn then remove immediately. Squeeze lemon juice over scallops. Sauté spinach in pan remove and drain.

To assemble dress salad and divide into portions then place in the centre of the plates. Evenly space artichokes in a circle around the salad. On top of each artichoke, place in the following order, firstly a small amount of spinach, then one scallop, half a teaspoon of aioli and finally a small shard of speck.

Place a small amount of sauterne sauce between each scallop and serve.

Courgette

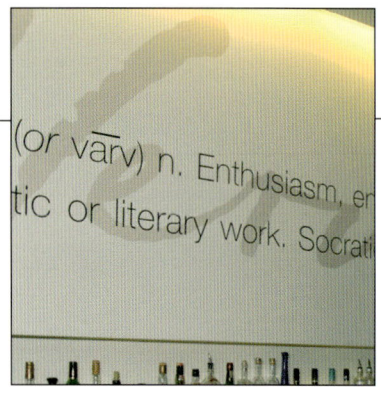

kangaroo fillets with blueberry pesto

200 g kangaroo fillets
roquette
baby spinach leaves
bulgarian fetta, crumbed
semi dried tomatoes
olive oil

blueberry pesto
180 g semi dried blueberries
60 g cashews – lightly roasted
sea salt
1 tablespoon grated parmesan
1 teaspoon mint
1 tablespoon parsley
1 lemon juiced
250 ml extra virgin olive oil

kangaroo fillet
Thread strips of kangaroo fillet onto skewers and grill until medium rare to allow kangaroo to remain moist and tender

blueberry pesto
Blend all ingredients using a mortar and pestle. Add olive oil slowly, blending well. Taste and season.

to serve
Place salad of roquette, baby spinach leaves, bulgarian fetta and semi dried tomatoes on plates, lightly dress with olive oil. Arrange skewers of kangaroo fillet on salad and place a spoonful of pesto on top. Serves 4

Verve

beef and caramelised onion grilled foccacia

1kg prime beef fillet
1 foccacia wheel cut into 8 wedges
4 sliced onions
1 cup white vinegar
1 cup brown sugar
½ teaspoon sweet ground paprika
1 teaspoon chilli flakes
dijon mustard
sea salt
freshly cracked pepper
olive oil
lettuce

beef
Season beef with sea salt and freshly cracked pepper. Rub with olive oil and roast in a preheated oven at 180°c for 40 minutes until rare. Set aside to cool.

caramelised Onions
Simmer onions, vinegar, sugar, chilli flakes and paprika in a deep frying pan, uncovered for 30 minutes or until thickened. Set aside to cool.

to serve
Cut foccacia wedges in half and toast. Spread with Dijon mustard. Fold beef slices and place on bottom half of foccacia, season with sea salt and freshly cracked pepper. Top with caramelised onions, crisp lettuce leaves and top half of foccacia.

Rolls Choice

jc69

muddle the following:

3 Wedges of Lemon

3 Lychees

45ml Bombay Sapphire Gin

15ml Paraiso Lychee Liqueur

10ml Campari

Shake and strain into a chilled martini glass, garnish with a lemon twist.

Academy

*The earth is waking
and a celebration of life begins*

Floriade

Pastel blossoms dance with the spring winds

summer

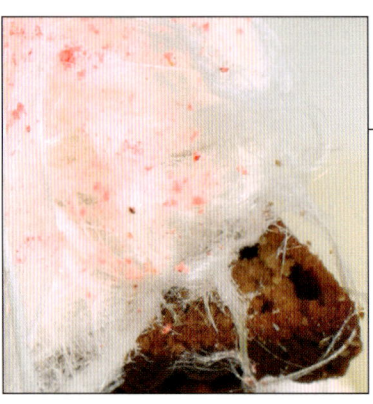
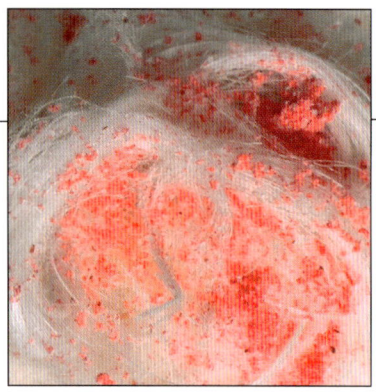

toasted gingerbread and coconut sorbet mille-feuille

gingerbread
225 g flour
½ teaspoon bicarb
¼ teaspoon salt
¼ teaspoon ground ginger
¼ teaspoon allspice
150 g treacle
150 ml milk
80 g unsalted butter
1 egg yolk

coconut sorbet
1 tablespoon glucose
400 ml sugar syrup
600 ml coconut milk
2 teaspoons rum
persian fairy floss
powdered strawberries

gingerbread
Sift all dry ingredients together. Heat butter, milk and treacle until butter melts. Mix with beaten egg yolk. Add sifted dry ingredients. Bake in a loaf tin at 180°c for 30–40 minutes. Cool, then slice 2mm thick. Toast in 180°c oven for 2–3 minutes. Cool.

sorbet
Process all ingredients in an ice cream machine.

Place ginger bread topped with sorbet on a plate, stacked three high. Garnish with Persian fairy floss and powdered strawberries.

The Ginger Room

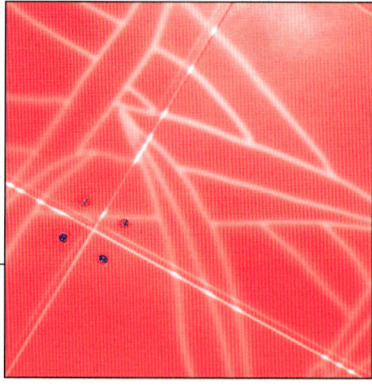

pan fried salmon with mediterranean vegetables and tomato relish

4x180 g salmon steaks
150 ml olive oil
splash of lemon juice
1 zucchini
1 egg plant
1 red capsicum
1 green capsicum
1 yellow capsicum
1 spanish onion
16 olives
16 cubes fetta
50 ml olive oil

Rub capsicums in olive oil and lay out on a tray. Place in oven at 220°c until skin peels off. Wash zucchini and cut in half down the middle. Peel Spanish onion and cut in half. When capsicums are ready, peel off the skin and gently break in half. Slice eggplant 1.5cm thick and salt. Leave for 10 minutes then wash the salt off.

Char grill the capsicums, zucchini, onions and eggplant till half cooked then place in an oven at 160°c for 10 minutes. When cooked cut capsicum into strips, onions in half and zucchini into bite sized pieces. Place all grilled vegetables in a large bowl, drizzle with olive oil and a squeeze of lemon. Season with salt and pepper and give a good toss. Set aside.

In a non stick pan heat up olive oil. Place salmon in pan and sear on both sides until golden brown. Finish cooking in an oven at 200°c for 7–10 minutes until medium rare.

tomato relish

Dice tomatoes and onions. Heat up a pot and add olive oil, onions and mustard seeds. Cook on low heat for 5 minutes. Turn up heat, add vinegar and reduce by half. Add tomatoes and stir. Cook for 20 minutes on high heat until tomatoes are soft and thick. Season and set aside to cool.

to serve

Carefully stack the grilled vegetables and fetta. Place salmon on top and finish with a spoonful of tomato relish and a teaspoon of yogurt. Drizzle olive oil around the plate. Serves 4

Belluci's

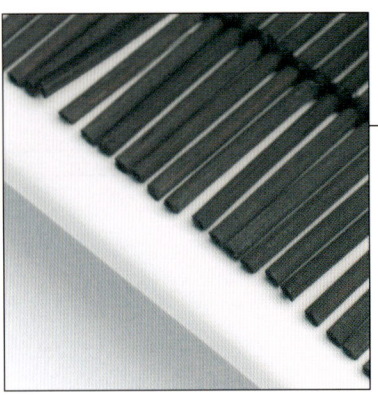

green apple muffins with gorgonzola soufflé

muffins
½ small green apple, grated for mix
½ small green apple, julienne for top
1 cup plain flour
1½ teaspoon baking powder
40 g parmesan grated
¼ cup milk
1 egg lightly beaten
30 ml olive oil
seasoning

soufflé
50 g gorgonzola
50 g ricotta
1 egg
salt
pepper

muffins
Sift flour and baking powder, add apple and parmesan, season. Make a well, fold in milk, eggs and oil. Don't overmix.

Bake in a well greased mini muffin tin at 180°c for 10–15 minutes, until skewer comes out clean. Cut off top when cooled to form a flat top.

soufflé
Mix gorgonzola, ricotta, salt and pepper together. Whisk egg white until stiff and then add to mixture.

Bake in mini muffin tins at 180°c for 10–15 minutes. Turn out to cool. Place on top of muffin and garnish with apple julienne.

Bookplate

hoi nam king prawns

12 king prawns
½ onion
½ green capsicum
½ red capsicum
2 shallot stems
4 crushed garlic
1 stem thai basil
2 hot chillies

sauce
1 tablespoon hot chilli oil
1 tablespoon chilli paste
  with soya bean oil
1 tablespoon fish sauce
1 tablespoon coconut milk
1 tablespoon palm sugar
1/3 cup water or chicken stock

Put a dash of cooking oil into a wok. Add garlic, hot chilli, chilli paste, king prawns and stir fry until the prawns turn red.

Add fish sauce, coconut milk, palm sugar and the chicken stock. Stir for a few seconds.

Add the green and red capsicum, basil and shallots stirring until all the sauce is absorbed.

Serve on a bed of boiled rice, with steamed fresh asian greens.

Portia's

spatchcock roasted with garlic lemon and rosemary on wild rice pilaf

4 spatchcocks, size 5
1 lemon
4 sprigs rosemary
8 garlic cloves

wild rice pilaf
1 tablespoons olive oil
40 g butter
4 eschallots, finely chopped
3 garlic cloves, finely chopped
4 thyme sprigs, finely chopped
2 bay leaves
50 ml white wine
1 cup long grain rice, well washed
¼ cup wild rice
1 ½ cup chicken stock
spinach

Preheat the oven to 180°c. Cut the lemon into 4 wedges, crush the garlic cloves whole with the flat side of a knife. Open up the cavity of the bird and place one lemon wedge, 2 garlic cloves and a rosemary sprig in each one. Season well with salt and pepper inside and out. Lay on a baking tray and drizzle each one with olive oil. Roast for 20 minutes then rest for 10. While the spatchcocks are resting deglaze the roasting tray with some white wine and lemon juice, reduce by half and add 200ml of chicken stock reduce by half again and strain through a fine sieve. When ready to serve whisk in a little butter to the sauce and correct the seasoning.

pilaf
Heat the butter and oil in a pot with a tight fitting lid that is suitable to go in the oven. Sautee the eschallots, garlic and herbs until softened but not coloured. Add the rices and stir to coat with the oil. Add the wine, chicken stock and season with salt and pepper. Bring to the boil and put on the lid. Bake in a 180°c oven for 15 minutes or until the rice is cooked and the stock has been absorbed.

to serve
Carve the legs and breasts off the spatchcocks and add any juices that come out of the inside to the sauce. Make a neat mound or press into a cutter some of the rice pilaf, top with some wilted spinach and the carved spatchcocks pour around some sauce and serve.

Atlantic

eastern king prawn eggnet with cucumber relish

egg net
4 eggs
salt
white pepper

filling
100 g bean sprouts
16 very large king prawns– uncooked, peeled and devained)
2 lime leaves shredded
1 stem lemongrass, finely chopped
½ bunch coriander leaves
½ bunch mint leaves
1 red chilli, deseeded and finely chopped
1 tablespoon roasted peanuts chopped
1 tablespoon peanut oil

cucumber relish
100 ml white vinegar
100 g white sugar
1 lebanese cucumber, seeded and sliced
2 golden shallots sliced
1 chilli, seeded and sliced

egg net
Beat eggs with salt and white pepper and strain into a bottle with a fine nozzle cap, like sauce bottle. Heat a large frying pan. Add 1 tablespoon of peanut oil. When hot drizzle the egg in a slow steady stream over a medium heat into a net like pattern.

filling
Heat wok and add peanut oil, heat to just smoking and fry prawns until pink coloured. Add chilli then other ingredients, toss over high heat until herbs are coloured bright green and sprouts are limp—do not overcook. Roll up while hot in the egg net and serve with relish.

relish
Heat vinegar and stir in sugar to dissolve. Cool. Pour over other ingredients. Serve in a side dish. Serves 4

The Ginger Room

banana tarte tatin

Ingredients per person
buttered puff pastry
100 g sugar
50 g butter
1 banana

In a pan over low heat slowly melt sugar, stirring intermediately until you have a caramel liquid. Add butter and stir until dissolved. You have made butterscotch.

Pour butterscotch into a heavy based pan, you will need the butterscotch liquid to be at least 1½cm deep in the pan.

Place bananas on top of butterscotch, you will need to cut the bananas 3 cm high and place upright in pan. Fill base of pan with bananas ensuring you leave a 1cm gap at the outer rim of the pan.

Cut puff pastry 4cm larger than the base of the pan, lay puff over bananas pressing excess puff between pan and bananas. Bake in 180°c oven for 20 minutes. Allow to cool for one hour.

Reheat tarte tatin for 20 minutes at 180°c. Turn out on plate, be careful as the liquid comes out of the pan, this is your sauce. Serve with vanilla ice-cream.

Waters Edge

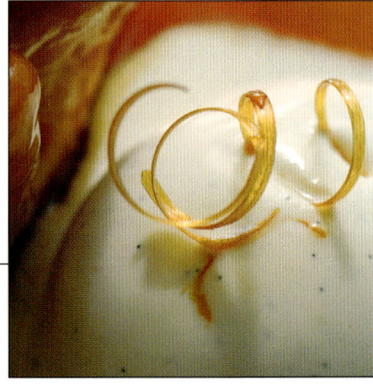

spaghetti marinara

250 ml white wine
pinch saffron
1 kg mussels
4 baby octopus
500 g prawns
500 g mixed fish
6 tomatoes
400g spaghetti
4 tablespoons olive oil
3 garlic cloves, crushed
500 g calamari
6 tablespoons parsley
lemon wedges

Place wine and saffron in a bowl and leave to infuse. Clean mussels by scrubbing them thoroughly. Rinse well under water. Place them in a large saucepan, cover pan and cook them for approximately 1–2 minutes or until they open. Discard any that don't open.

Clean octopus by slitting the head and pulling out the innards. Cut out the eyes and hard beak then rinse. Lie the calamari out flat and score a criss cross pattern in the flesh. Slice diagonally into 2 x 4 cm strips. Peel and devein the prawns.

Score a cross on top of each tomato and then plunge them into boiling water for 20 seconds, drain and peel away the skin from the cross, then core and chop. Cook the pasta in a large pan of boiling salted water until al dente.

Heat the oil in a frypan and add garlic and tomato. Stir over moderate heat for 10-15 seconds then pour in saffon infused wine. Season and simmer for 8-10 minutes until reduced by half. Add in all of the seafood to cook.

Drain the spaghetti and return to the pan. Add ⅔ of the sauce, toss well then transfer to a large serving platter. Spoon the remaining sauce over the top and serve with lemon wedge. Serves 4

Tossolini's

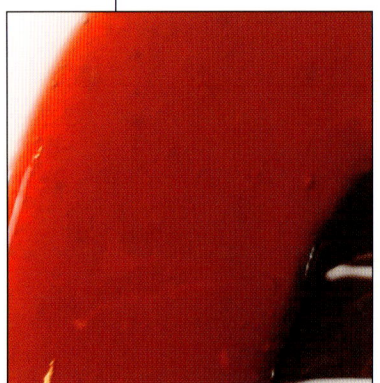

flourless chocolate cake

cake
400 g chocolate
2 tablespoons brandy
2 tablespoons coffee
200 g butter
200 g castor sugar
200 g almond meal
6 eggs separated
½ teaspoon baking powder

white chocolate
250 g white chocolate
250 ml pouring cream

chocolate gavanche
500 ml cream
500 g bitter couverture chocolate

raspberry coulis
water
sugar
250 g rasberries

cake
Combine chocolate, brandy and coffee in a heat proof bowl and melt until well combined. Add sugar and butter, remove from heat and add almond meal, then egg yolks. Beat the egg whites until stiff. Gradually fold the whites into the chocolate mix. Pour into small non stick moulds and bake at 180°c for 35–45 minutes, or until cooked. Cool in tin before turning out.

chocolate gavanche
Bring cream to the boil and then add chocolate whilst boiling, whisk together and then pour over individual cakes.

white chocolate
Bring cream to the boil, add chocolate stirring until it thickens. Pour a spoonful over individual cakes

raspberry coulis
Mix equal parts water and sugar to make a syrup, add raspberries and bring to the boil. Pour mixture into a sieve and pass mixture through to separate any pips. Coulis should be runny in consistency but not a thick liquid.

Tossolini's

January 2003

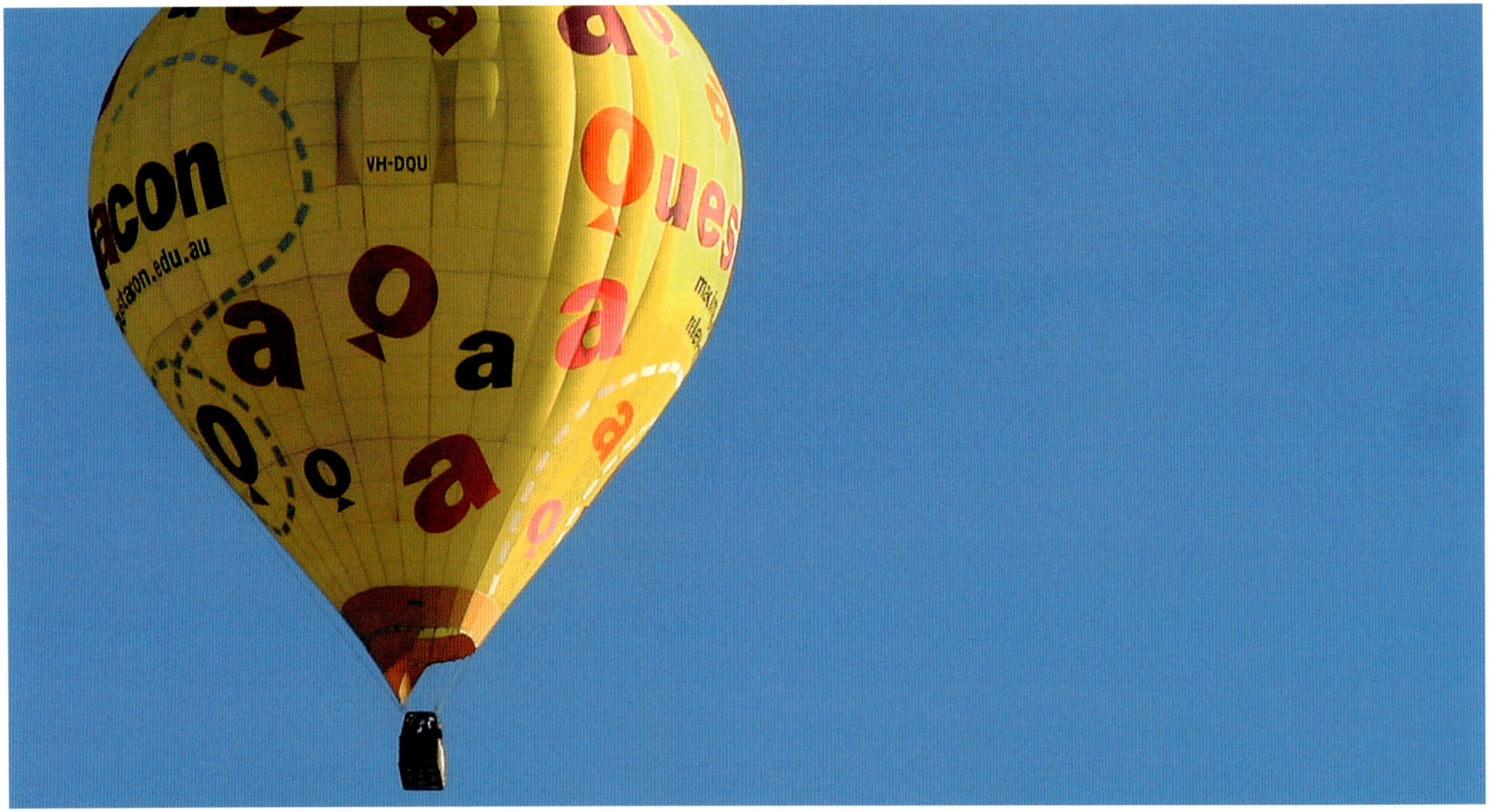
VH-DQU

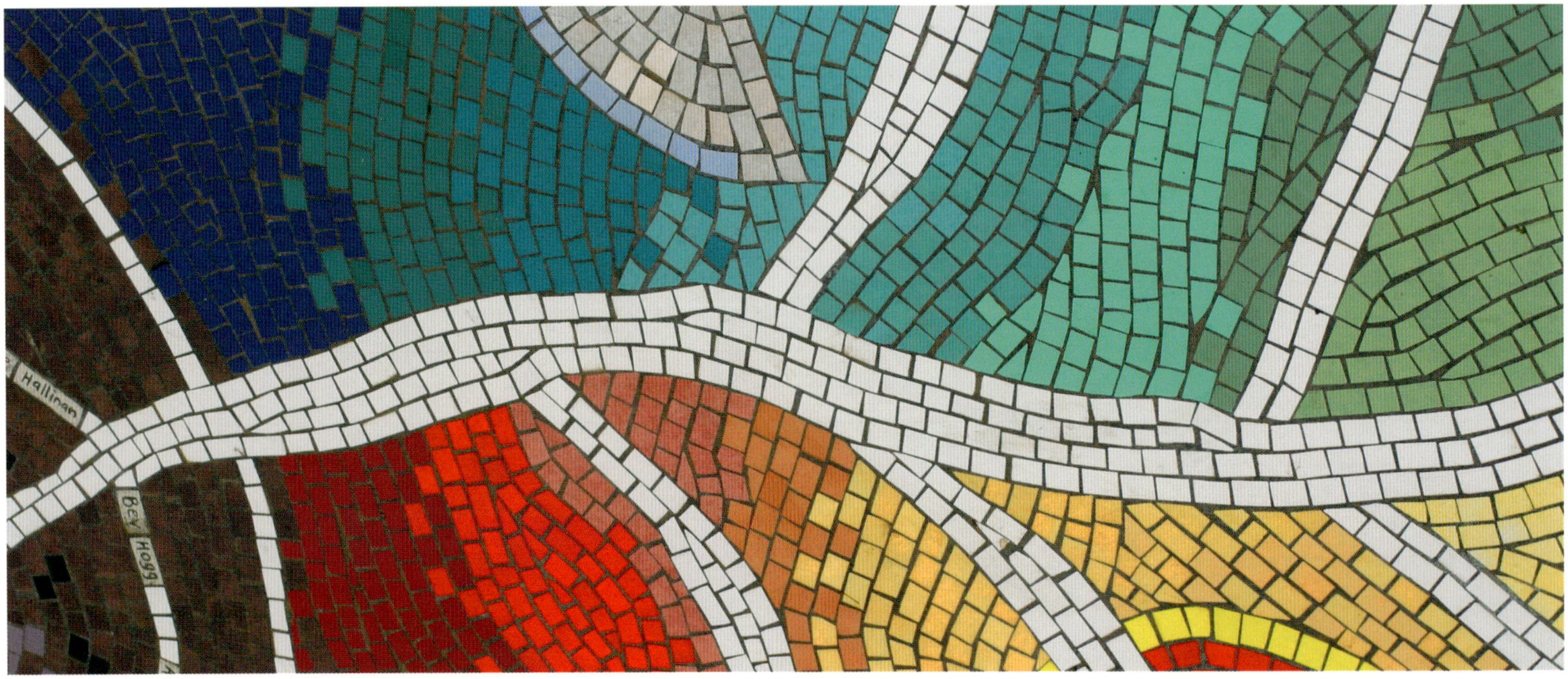
Hallinan
Bev Hogg

Cornucopia

autumn

roasted butternut pumpkin tart with crème fraiche and onion marmalade

tart
1 small butternut pumpkin
1 sheet of puff pastry
100 ml fresh tomato sauce
100 ml crème fraiche or sour cream

onion marmalade
1 onion sliced (200gm)
2 teaspoon salt
100 ml white wine vinegar
100 g sugar
pinch caraway seeds

Cut pastry into 4 rounds and bake at 200°c for 7–10 minutes. Remove and cool. Peel, seed and slice pumpkin. Brush the pumpkin with oil and roast at 180°c for 10-15 minutes until tender.

Sprinkle salt on sliced onion and leave for 1 hour. Rinse with cold water and drain. Put onions, vinegar, sugar and caraway seed in a saucepan and cook slowly till golden brown and the syrup thickens. Set aside to cool.

Place pastry round on a metal tray and spread a little tomato sauce on each pastry, then place pumpkin on top. Bake at 200°c for 5–7 minutes. Place on warm plates with crème fraiche and onion marmalade. Serves 4

Anise

eggplant and smoked tomato ratatouille with smoked lamb cutlets

12 poachers pantry smoked lamb cutlets
100 g salad leaves (wild roquette)

ratatouille

2 large brown onions
2 cloves garlic
¼ cup olive oil
1 large eggplant, diced into 2cm cubes
2 zucchini, diced into 2 cm cubes
1 red capsicum, diced into 2 cm cubes
6 diced Italian tomatoes
200 g poachers pantry smoked tomatoes, cut into large dice
3 tablespoons tomato puree
2 tablespoons tiny capers
¼ cup pitted black olives
½ bunch fresh basil
sea salt
freshly ground black pepper

aioli

3 egg yolks
2 cloves garlic
2-3 tablespoons fresh lemon juice
300 ml olive oil
sea salt
freshly ground black pepper

ratatouille

In a medium sized saucepan sauté finely diced onions and crushed garlic in olive oil until slightly coloured, to the pan add eggplant, zucchini, red capsicum, fresh tomatoes, smoked tomatoes, tomato puree, capers and olives. Cook over low heat until eggplant is soft. Adjust seasoning with sea salt and fresh cracked pepper. Stir through finely shredded basil leaves to finish. Serve warm or at room temperature

aioli

In a food processor blend the egg yolks with a pinch of salt, garlic and lemon juice to taste. Slowly add the olive oil to make mayonnaise. Adjust the seasoning

lamb cutlets

Panfry, char grill or bbq smoked lamb cutlets for 4 minutes each side, or until slightly caramel in colour.

to serve

Place some salad greens in the centre of plates, top with ratatouille and three smoked cutlets. Garnish with some aioli and fresh basil leaves. Serves 4

Poacher's Pantry

sauté morton bay bug tails with braised oxtail and truffle jus

500 g oxtail
2 carrots chopped
2 onions chopped
2 garlic cloves
pinch fresh thyme
1 tablespoon tomato paste
1 litre veal stock
2 bug tails
500 ml veal jus
1 teaspoon truffle paste
pinch chopped parsley
hand full diced tomato
sea salt
freshly ground black pepper
oil for cooking

oxtail
In a medium pot sauté on high heat with 1 tablespoon of oil, carrots, onions, garlic, thyme and tomato paste, set aside for a moment. Season oxtail with salt and pepper then seal on a hot pan with 2 tablespoons of oil. Place oxtail in a pot with the roasted vegetables and cover with veal stock. Bring to the boil and then place in a moderate oven for 2 hours or until soft and tender. Once cooked strain off liquid keeping aside for rehydrating. Pick oxtail off the bone and disregard and fatty bits.

sauce
Heat veal jus in a sauce pot. Mix in truffle paste, diced tomato and parsley.

bugs
Season bugs with salt and pepper, heat a non–stick pan add 1 teaspoon oil and sauté bugs until cooked.

to serve
Place oxtail in centre of plate, using a ring cutter. Place bug tail on top and sauce with truffle jus.

Aubergine

tortellini di zucca – ricotta, pumpkin and leek tortellini with burnt sage butter

pasta dough
600 g OO doppio flour
3 eggs
125 ml water
85 ml olive oil
pinch salt

filling
500g butternut pumpkin, peeled and cut into 5cm cubes
300 g leek, trimmed
300 g fresh ricotta
50 g butter
freshly ground black pepper
sea salt

burnt sage butter
100 g unsalted butter
20 g sage leaves, finely chopped
freshly ground black pepper
sea salt

pasta
Combine all the ingredients into a mixing bowl at low speed, starting with the flour, eggs, olive oil, water and salt until the dough comes together. This may take up to 20 minutes. Add flour or water if needed depending on the consistency of the dough. The pasta dough should not be wet and soft. Once combined well, remove and cover and place in a cool dry place for resting.

filling
In a pan add the butter, roast pumpkin and leek cooking until coloured. Allow to cool and add the ricotta and season. Combine and process in a food processor until pureed. Push the filling through a sieve into a bowl.

burnt sage butter
Combine the ingredients into warm pan over heat until brown in colour, almost burnt.

Using a pasta maker roll out dough to the thinnest setting. Cut the pasta into 6cm squares. Place a teaspoon of cooled pumpkin filling in the centre of each square and fold over diagonally, pressing down the sides firmly with egg wash. Then stretch over the other two corners together to form a delicate round parcel shape pasta. Dust with semolina and place in boiling water. Once the pasta surfaces, it is cooked (3-5 minutes). Drain and toss through the sage butter and finish with grated parmesan.
Serves 4

Mezzalira

Bookplate

lemon and oregano marinated lamb fillet on crisp kataifi pastry with fetta mint and vine ripened tomato salsa

60 g butter
1 packet kataifi pastry
2–3 lamb fillets

marinade
½ preserved lemon skin, finely diced
1 teaspoon dried greek oregano
vegetable oil
sea salt
freshly ground pepper
finely chopped garlic

salsa
1 vine ripened tomato,
  seeded and finely diced
70 g good quality greek fetta,
  finely diced
1 teaspoon finely chopped mint
extra virgin olive oil
finely ground black pepper

Trim lamb fillet and marinate overnight.

Take a small amount of kafaifi pastry and moisten with melted butter. Press into 4cm round pastry cutter and press down firmly until flat.

Repeat until you have enough bases. Bake until golden brown at 180°c for 15–20 minutes.

In a hot pan add a tablespoon of oil and cook off the lamb fillets until pink, turning frequently. Allow to rest before cutting and placing side up on the pastry bases.

Combine all salsa ingredients and spoon on top of lamb. Serve warm.

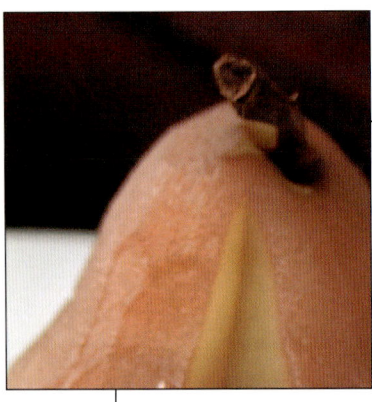

poached pear stuffed with rhubarb & blueberry compote

poached pears
4 green pears, peeled and cored
red cooking wine
200 g sugar
2 cinnamon sticks
6 star anise whole

stuffing
1 bunch rhubarb
100 g sugar
2 punnet fresh blueberries
10 g butter
200 ml liquid reserved
   from poached pears

butterscotch sabayon
6 egg yolks
150 g sugar
150 ml butterscotch schnapps

poached pears
Place pears in a saucepan deep enough to cover but fit fruit snugly. Add sufficient wine to cover pears, add sugar, cinnamon and anise and bring to boil. Simmer till pears are tender but firm (approx 30 min). Let cool in poaching liquid, drain and reserve liquid for compote

stuffing
Slice rhubarb into 1 inch lengths. Heat a heavy based pan, melt butter and sauté rhubarb till slightly coloured. Add sugar and caramelise. Add reserved poaching liquid and simmer till rhubarb is tender and liquid is mostly reduced. Take off heat and add blueberries

butterscotch sabayon
In a large stainless steel bowl, cream together yolks and sugar till light and fluffy. Add butterscotch schnapps and cook over low heat, whisking continuously till mixture starts to thicken

to serve
Leaving pears whole, fill with warm rhubarb compote and serve butterscotch sabayon on the side. Garnish with extra stuffing. Serves 4

Milk and Honey

assiette of pork with caramelised pears

6 quality pork sausages
1 pork hock
1 smoked pork hock
5 gelatine leaves
½ kg pork belly
6 slices of blood pudding
6 scallops
6 pork trotters
veal stock
chicken stock
hickory
6 quail eggs
2 pears
100 g butter
100 g brown sugar
400 ml muscat
onions
celery
garlic
thyme
bay leaf

hock terrine
Bring hock and smoked hock to the boil, discard water and cover hocks with ½ chicken stock and ½ water. Bring to the boil and skim. Add onions, leeks, celery, garlic, thyme and bay leaf and simmer until meat falls off the bone.

Pick through meat, and place in a bowl. To 300ml of hock stock add 5 leaves of gelatine. Add hocks and set in a terrine mould overnight. Retain the rest of the stock for sauce.

pork belly
Slowly roast pork belly at 160°c oven for 3–4 hours. When cold, slice pork 1cm thick and 4cm long – serve with blood pudding and seared scallops.

smoked trotter
Braise trotters in beef stock with herbs for up to 6 hours at 160°c. For the stuffing combine trimmings of pork sausage, belly, hock and blood pudding. Remove skins from trotters and lay out on cling film. Steam for 25 minutes and then wrap tightly in foil. Refrigerate overnight. Lightly smoke with hickory in a camp smoker and refrigerate, slice 1cm thick and pan fry. Serve with fried quail egg.

caramelised pears
Bring butter and brown sugar up to the boil and add diced pears. Sauté on a medium heat until caramelised.

to make sauce
Reduce 100ml muscat and then add 500ml of the saved hock stock and bring to the boil, skim the fat and simmer for a further 10 minutes then pass through a fine strainer.

to plate
Pan fry trotters, pork belly, seared scallops, blood pudding and sausage, in a separate pan fry a quail egg.

Place quail egg on trotter, blood pudding and scallops on pork belly, arrange pears in centre of plate and sauce over ingredients.
Drizzle a good olive oil over the top and serve.

Waters Edge

baked apple with brioche pudding and maple syrup

6 slices brioche loaf
100 g sugar
3 egg yolks
3 whole eggs
250 ml cream
butter
vanilla
6 pink lady apples
150 g brioche crumbs
50 g melted butter
2 teaspoons cinnamon
maple syrup
cream

Whisk eggs with sugar then add cream and vanilla to form the custard. Lightly butter brioche slices and layer into a baking dish. Pour over the custard. Bake in a bainmarie filled with water at 160°c for 30 minutes until set. Cool and then cut into neat squares of pudding.

Combine crumbs, sugar, butter and cinnamon. Spoon into the centre of the cored apples. Brush with butter and sprinkle with sugar. Bake at 220°c for 20 minutes or until apples are soft and coloured.

Reheat pudding squares, top with apples and pour over maple syrup and cream.

Silo

chocolate, whiskey and ricotta cheesecake

pastry base
350 g unsalted butter
155 g icing sugar
4 egg yolks
500 g plain flour
50 ml cold water

filling
800 g neufchatel cheese
100 g ricotta
3 eggs
zest one lemon
225 g castor sugar
1 teaspoon vanilla essence
3 tablespoons cornflour
400 g milk chocolate
200 ml pouring cream
100 ml whiskey

pastry

In a whiz mix butter and sugar. Add the egg yolks one at a time. Add flour and a little water just so pastry starts to lump. Tip into a bowl, knead together slightly. Wrap pastry in gladwrap and refrigerate for one hour.

Roll out pastry into a circle on baking paper allowing for shrinkage, bake in 160°c oven for 30 minutes.

Cut to fit 8–10 inch cake tin. Reduce oven to 120°c.

filling

Whiz cheeses together until soft. In mixer beat eggs, zest, sugar, vanilla and cornflour. Add cheeses and continue beating.

Melt chocolate over a pot of boiling water.

Add cream, whiskey and melted chocolate to cheese mix and beat until well combined.

Pour into cake tin on pastry base and bake for 25–30 minutes. Filling will not be firm. Turn oven off and leave in oven for a further 15 minutes. Refrigerate overnight, serve the next day garnished with a brandy snap, scoop of ice-cream and a drizzle of melted chocolate.

Green Herring

White frosty mist begins to hang low over the lake

Translucent still water is covered in liquid crystal

Lest we forget

Sunset lingers and burns the sky flames dissolve gradually

*As you walk along
the lakeshore at sunset
the gentle sounds
of the Carillon bells echo
across the water*

winter

madgery creek venison, braised red cabbage, celeriac puree and port jus

1 venison fillet
8 king trumpet mushrooms
100 g baby spinach, washed
1 brown onion, sliced
4 garlic cloves, sliced
50 g speck
¼ red cabbage, finely sliced
1 bay leaf
4 thyme stalks
100 ml red wine vinegar
100 g brown sugar
1 celeriac
1 potato
butter
milk
water
1 cup port
1 cup veal jus

Sweat the onions, garlic and speck. Add cabbage, herbs, vinegar and sugar. Bring to simmer, season and put in oven at 180°c for approx 90–120 minutes. Stir and check every 20 minutes. Finished product should be deep purple in colour and quite sticky.

Peel and dice celeriac and potato, place in a saucepan and cover with equal amounts of milk and water. Add a knob of butter and season with salt. Cook till soft. Pour off liquid and puree. Add butter and seasoning to taste.

In a saucepan reduce port until sticky add veal jus and reduce to a glaze.

Sear venison and cook to rare, leave to rest. Sauté the mushrooms and spinach (separately). Serve celeriac puree on to plate in a moon shape to one side, place spinach on other side. Slice venison and place on spinach. Pile cabbage in the middle with mushrooms on top. Pour sauce over meat and serve.

Courgette

brasato di anatra—braised duck with ligurian olives, cavolo nero and celeriac gratinata

4 duck maryland (size 24 duck)
300 g ligurian olives
4 sprigs thyme
4 cloves garlic, crushed
1 litre chicken stock
250 ml dry white wine
30ml olive oil
1 kg celeriac
400 ml cream
maldon rock salt
freshly cracked black pepper
400g cavolo nero (black italian cabbage)

Pre heat oven to 170°c. Salt duck generously and leave for 30 minutes. In a hot pan, add the olive oil and quickly seal the duck on both sides and remove. Place duck in a deep braising dish and add the olives, thyme, garlic, stock and enough wine to just cover the duck. Place in oven and cook for 1 hour 45 minutes. Once cooked, allow to rest for 8–10 minutes in a warm place.

gratinata
Peel and slice celeriac using a mandolin into thin slices. Line baking dish with silicon paper and layer with sliced celeriac, seasoning each layer with salt and pepper. Pour cream over covering the top layer. Bake in oven at 170°c for 45 minutes.

to serve
Cut gratinata into 4 pieces and place wilted cavolo nero and duck on top. Pour in the cooking liquid along with thyme and olives. Serves 4

Mezzalira

roast pumpkin prosciutto and sage risotto

18 thin slices prosciutto
½ cup sage leaves
50 g butter
450 g peeled pumpkin chunks
extra virgin olive
1 litre chicken stock
2 large brown onions
3 cloves garlic
160 g butter
¼ cup extra virgin olive oil
750 g arborio rice
½ cup fresh shaved parmesan
sea salt
freshly ground black pepper

Preheat oven to 200°c, brush the pumpkin with extra extra virgin olive oil and bake for 25 minutes. Crisp the prosciutto and sage leaves, dotted with 50g butter on separate trays for 12 minutes.

Bring the stock to the boil then reduce to a simmer. Finely chop the onions and garlic, sauté them with 100g of the butter and ¼ cup extra virgin olive oil until almost translucent. Turn up the heat and add the rice, stirring until well coated and gleaming. Reduce the heat and add the first ladle full of stock, stirring to incorporate it. Continue cooking, adding a ladleful of stock as the last is absorbed and stirring all the while. The rice takes about 20 minutes to cook and should not go beyond al dente.

Crumble the prosciutto and stir through the risotto with the parmesan, pumpkin, sage and butter reserving a little sage and prosciutto for garnish. Serve with fresh parmesan

Poacher's Pantry

venison pie, roasted loin and raspberry cabernet sauce

pastry
250 g flour
50 g almond meal
125 g butter
50 g shredded cheddar

pie mix
1 stick celery
1 red onion
3 thyme sprigs
freshly ground black pepper
200 ml port
400 ml stock
400 g diced venison
200 g blueberries
2 tablespoons cornflour

sauce
500 ml red wine
200 ml port
500 ml venison or beef stock
100 ml raspberry puree
cornflour
4 x 100 g venison loin pieces
butter
200 g baby spinach leaves

pastry
Blend all ingredients in a kitchen whiz. When turned to fine crumbs tip into a large bowl. Add enough cold water to bind together and form into a ball. Knead with a little extra plain flour for 5 minutes then cover and set aside for 1 hour.

pie mix
Finely chop celery and onion. Sauté in a splash of oil with thyme and fresh ground pepper. Add port and stock and bring to the boil, then turn down to a simmer. In a separate pan sauté diced venison in small batches and then add to the simmering liquid. Add blueberries and salt and simmer for 1 hour or until meat is tender, stir occasionally. When meat is tender, thicken slightly with cornflour mixed with a little water. Set aside to cool.

to assemble
Divide pastry ball into smaller balls about the size of a squash ball, then roll into thin rounds. Line 4 buttered moulds with a piece of pastry, leaving a large overlap all around. Fill with pie mix and fold overlap together, press and seal. Put on a tray and bake a 180°c oven for 30 minutes.

sauce
In a large pot bring red wine to the boil and reduce by half. Add port and stock, then reduce by half. Add raspberry puree, bring back to the boil then thicken slightly with cornflour. Remove from heat and set aside until needed.

the last furious 10 minutes…
Sear the venison loins in a pan with a little butter. Put on a tray and place in a 180°c oven for 5 minutes, pull out and rest in a warm spot for 6 minutes. Add a little more butter to the pan to heat. Throw in the spinach and move quickly around the pan to wilt. Place spinach on kitchen paper then onto a plate. Turn out pie and put at the other end of the plate. Slice loin and place on spinach. Pour sauce over pie and drizzle over loin and around plate. Drizzle a little sour cream over loin and garnish plate, if you have fresh raspberries scatter them around the plate, serve and eat with gusto!

Green Herring

"I love venison. There are so many ways to cook, serve and enjoy this versatile meat. This dish puts a slow cooked and a fast cooked element together that are great separate but unite wonderfully.

In the 17 years we have had the restaurant we have cooked venison so many ways with so many flavour combinations, these are mere drops in the ocean of game cuisine..."

roast chicken breast with chicken mushroom sauce

½ chicken per person
exotic mushrooms, sauté
2 shallots
2 large garlic cloves
chicken stock
cream
white wine
dry mushrooms
pasta sheets

chicken ravioli

Roast chicken legs off in advance, when cool, pull from bone and remove skin, chop in to fine pieces. Roast sauté mushrooms in a pan, reserve some for garnish, chop the rest and add to chicken leg meat. Combine and season. Make the raviolis with the pre made pasta sheets from a reputable deli.

sauce

In a warm pan sauté dry mushrooms with sliced onions and one clove of garlic for 5–8 minutes then add 200 ml white wine, reduce by ¾ then add 500ml chicken stock and reduce by half. Add 250 ml cream and bring to the boil. Season and pass through a fine sieve.

Roast peeled shallots and remaining garlic in a moderate oven for approximately 20 minutes with olive oil, salt and pepper.

presentation

Brush chicken breast with olive oil and season. Roast in a hot oven until cooked. Cook ravioli in boiling water until they float to the surface. Bring the sauce to the boil and adjust seasoning, add chopped cloves.

Place ravioli on top of chicken breast in the centre of the plate. Arrange roasted shallots and garlic, sautéed mushrooms around the plate and sauce the chicken and serve.

Waters Edge

steamed vanilla pudding with slow braised quinces and anglaise sauce

vanilla puddings
3 eggs
100 g sugar
25 g butter
250 ml milk
5 ml vanilla extract
175 g self raising flour

slow braised quinces
6 quinces
1 litre orange juice
200 g sugar
1 vanilla pod, split in half
1 cinnamon stick
cloves
orange, zest and juice
lemon, juice

anglaise sauce
150ml milk
40g sugar
½ vanilla pod, split in half
2 egg yolks

vanilla puddings
Pre-heat oven to 170°c. Butter and sugar 6 individual pudding moulds and sit them in a deep baking tray. Boil the kettle. Whip the eggs and sugar until thick and pale. Fold in the melted butter then the vanilla and milk. Sift and gently fold in the flour. Pour into the prepared pudding moulds to just under the rim. Pour boiling water into the tray to a third of the way up the moulds. Cover the tray with cling film and then alfoil to form a tight seal. Bake in a 170°c oven for 20 to 25 minutes. Test with a skewer. When done it will come out clean. Allow to cool on the tray before storing.

quinces
Put all ingredients except the quinces in a deep non-reactive baking dish and bring to a simmer on the stove. Peel the quinces and cut in half, remove the cores and stems and place in the simmering liquid. you will need to top up the liquid with water to cover the quinces. Wrap with cling film and then with foil. Poach very gently for 4 to 8 hours at 120°c. Do not disturb the quinces while cooking as they are soft and prone to break up. If the liquid begins to boil turn the oven down a little and leave the door open until the heat is reduced. The quinces should go a deep red colour after 4 or 5 hours and if it is feasible turn the oven off and allow them to cool overnight in the oven. Refrigerate in the baking dish and when fully cold transfer into an airtight container, cover them with the liquid and reserve any excess liquid for other uses.

anglaise sauce
Warm the milk, sugar and vanilla pod. Stand for 15 minutes to infuse then scrape and squeeze all the seeds and flavour from the vanilla pod. Set up a bowl with ice and water that the pot will sit in. Whisk the infused milk into the egg yolks and return to the stove. Whisk over a low heat until it is nearly simmering and thickened. Cool immediately in the ice water to prevent it curdling.

to serve
Heat the puddings and the quinces in the microwave. Gently warm the anglaise sauce. Place cut quinces in the centre of a warm plate. Top with the pudding and pour around the anglaise sauce.

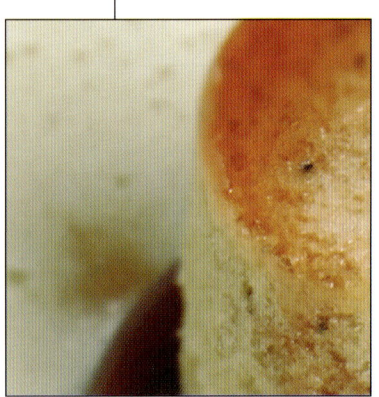

Atlantic

woodstock pizza

pizza dough
1 teaspoon active dry yeast
pinch sugar
⅔ cup warm water
2 cup plain flour
1 teaspoon sea salt
1 tablespoon olive oil

toppings
bacon
olives
oregano
capers
onion
cheese
fresh tomato sauce

Place yeast, sugar and water in a bowl. Set aside until bubbles form. Add the flour, salt and oil. Mix to form smooth dough and knead for 10 minutes or until smooth and elastic. Place in a clean, oiled bowl, cover and allow to stand in a warm place for 20 minutes or until doubled in size. Roll out to 21-3 mm thick and place on a pizza tray.

Spread fresh tomato sauce over base, then layer with fresh tomato and onion. Sprinkle generously with cheese. Cut bacon into 2 cm pieces and spread over. Finally top with fresh oregano and capers. Bake in a 220°c preheated oven until crust is golden and cheese melted.

baba's torte | БАБИНА ТОРТА

crepes	filling
2 eggs	400 g ground walnuts
400 g plain flour	250 g castor sugar
pinch salt	100 g currants
400 ml milk	100 g sultanas
	zest one lemon

Mix eggs with flour gradually adding the milk. Use whisk for smooth mixture. In a 20cm crepe pan make 12–15 crepes. For filling mix all ingredients together and set aside.

To put together use 22cm round oven proof dish layering one crepe then covering with filling, then another crepe etc until you run out.

Probe the cake with a knife and pour milk in.

Place in a pre heated oven at 180°c for about 30 minutes.

Serve warm with a dollop of double cream. Serves 8–12

The night sky turns into a silk sheet
of indigo black torn by stars

Cold winds whistle freely through the naked branches

In the distance the Brindabella's are dressed in white

Black Mountain towers over the city

Sculpture Garden

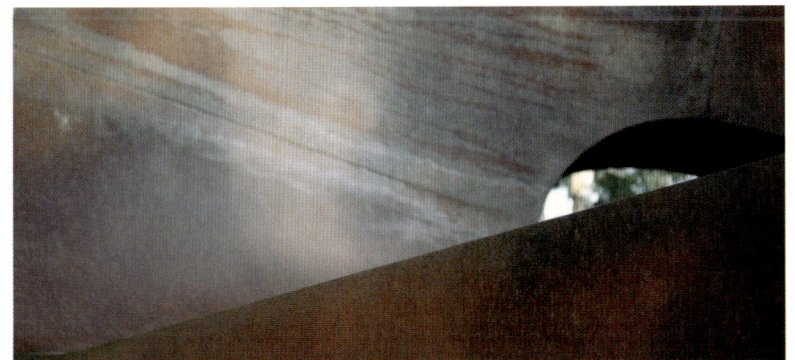

notes

restaurant index

Academy, Canberra City, 6257 3355 30
Anise, Canberra City, 6257 0700 .... 14, 80
Atlantic, Manuka, 6232 7888 .... 56, 124
Aubergine, Griffith ACT, 6260 8666 84
Belluci's, Woden, 6282 1700 50
Bookplate, National Library, Parkes ACT, 6262 1154 .... 18, 52, 88
Courgette, Canberra City, 6247 4042 .... 24, 114
Green Herring, Gold Creek Village, 6230 2657 .... 96, 120
Mezzalira, Canberra City, 6230 0025 .... 86, 116
Milk & Honey, Canberra City, 6247 7722 .... 20, 90
Ottoman Cuisine, Barton, 6273 6111 16
Poachers Pantry, Hall, 6230 2487 .... 82, 118
Portia's Place, Kingston, 6239 7970 54
Rolls Choice, Fyshwick, 6280 7058 28
Silo Bakery, Kingston, 6260 6060 94
The Ginger Room, Old Parliament House, Parkes, 6270 8262 .... 48, 58
Tosolini's, Canberra City, 6247 4317 .... 62, 64
Verve, Manuka, 6239 4666 .... 22, 26
Waters Edge, Parkes ACT, 6273 5066 .... 60, 92, 122
Woodstock, Canberra City, 6249 7969 126

photo index

Belluci's - Woden 11
Brindabella Ranges 138
Carillon 99, 106, 140
Commonwealth Avenue Bridge 36, 77, 104
Go Troppo - Fyshwick Markets 72
King's Avenue Bridge 140
Lotus Bay 101
National Library 36, 76, 106, 137
National Museum of Australia 74
Old Parliament House 33
Parkes Place Pontoon 107
Telstra Tower 8, 41, 139
Sculpture garden 142, 143
War Memorial 102

jeremy rozdarz

zorana grbic

recipe index

a
- apple, baked with brioche pudding and maple syrup 94
- apple, green muffins with gorgonzola soufflé 52
- assiette of pork with caramelized pears 92

b
- baba's torta 128
- baked apple with brioche pudding and maple syrup 94
- banana tarte tatin 60
- barramundi, oven roasted fillet of, on a fennel and orange salad 14
- braised duck with ligurian olives, cavolo nero and celeriac gatinata-brasato di anatra 116
- brasato di anatra-braised duck with ligurian olives, cavolo nero and celeriac gatinata 116
- butternut pumpkin, roasted tart with crème fraiche and onion marmalade 80

c
- cheesecake, chocolate, whiskey and ricotta 96
- chicken breast, roast with chicken mushroom sauce 122
- chicken, tandoori foccacia 28
- chocolate cake, flourless 64
- chocolate, whiskey and ricotta cheesecake 96
- cocktail - jc69 30
- cod, grilled chermoula marinated in vine leaves with cucumber and chilli dipping sauce 18

d
- duck, braised with ligurian olives, cavolo nero and celeria 58
- eggplant and smoked tomato ratatouille with smoked lamb cutlets 82

f
- flourless chocolate cake 64
- foccacia, tandoori chicken 28

g
- gingerbread, toasted and coconut sorbet mille-feuille 48
- green apple muffins with gorgonzola soufflé 52
- grilled chermoula marinated cod in vine leaves with cucumber and chilli dipping sauce 18

h
- hoi nam king prawns 54

j
- jc69 30

k
- kangaroo fillets with blueberry pesto 26
- king prawn, eastern, eggnet with cucumber relish 58
- king prawns, hoi nam 54

l
- lamb fillet, lemon and oregano marinated on crisp kataifi pastry with fetta mint and vine ripened tomato salsa . . . 88
- lamb rack, pistachio crumbed served with sweet potato mash 20
- lamb, smoked cutlets with eggplant and smoked tomato ratatouille 82
- lemon and oregano marinated lamb fillet on crisp kataifi pastry with fetta mint and vine ripened tomato salsa 88

m
- madgery creek venison, braised red cabbage, celeriac puree and port jus 114
- morton bay bug tails, sautéd with braised ox tail and truffle jus 84

recipe index

o
- oven roasted fillet of barramundi on a fennel and orange salad ... 14
- oxtail, braised with sauté morton bay bug tails and truffle jus ... 84

p
- pan fried salmon with mediterranean vegetables and tomato relish ... 50
- pear, poached, stuffed with rhubarb and blueberry compote served with butterscotch sabayon ... 90
- pistachio crumbed lamb rack served with sweet potato mash ... 20
- pizza, woodstock ... 126
- poached pear stuffed with rhubarb and blueberry compote served with butterscotch sabayon ... 90
- pork, assiette of with caramelized pears ... 92
- pumpkin, ricotta, and leek tortellini with burnt sage butter-tortellini di zucca ... 86
- ratatouille, eggplant and smoked tomato with smoked lamb cutlets ... 82
- risotto, roast pumpkin prosciutto and sage ... 118
- roast chicken breast with chicken mushroom sauce ... 122
- roast pumpkin prosciutto and sage risotto ... 118
- roast vegetable stack with polenta on creamed leeks and cannelini beans ... 22
- roasted butternut pumpkin tart with crème fraiche and onion marmalade ... 80

s
- salmon, pan fried with mediterranean vegetables and tomato relish ... 50
- sauté morton bay bug tails with braised ox tail and truffle jus ... 84
- scallops, seared 'spring bay' with jerusalem artichokes, crisp speck and sauternes butter sauce ... 24
- seared 'spring bay' scallops with jerusalem artichokes, crisp speck and sauternes butter sauce ... 24
- spaghetti marinara ... 62
- spatchcock roasted with garlic lemon and rosemary on wild rice pilaf ... 56
- steamed vanilla pudding with slow braised quinces and anglaise sauce ... 124

t
- tandoori chicken foccacia ... 28
- toasted gingerbread and coconut sorbet mille-feuille ... 48
- torta, baba's ... 128
- tortellini di zucca-ricotta, pumpkin and leek tortellini with burnt sage butter ... 86
- tuna tartare ... 16

v
- vanilla pudding, steamed with slow braised quinces and anglaise sauce ... 124
- vegetable stack, roast with polenta on creamed leeks and cannelini beans ... 22
- venison pie, roasted loin and raspberry cabernet sauce ... 120
- venison, madgery creek, braised red cabbage, celeriac puree and port jus ... 114

w
- woodstock pizza ... 126